Dropping In On...

EGYPT

Lewis K. Parker

A Geography Series

ROURKE BOOK COMPANY, INC.
VERO BEACH, FLORIDA 32964

Printed in the United States of America

Revised Edition 2004

Library of Congress Cataloging-in-Publication Data

Parker, Lewis K.
    Dropping in on Egypt / Lewis K. Parker.
      p.   cm. — (Dropping in on)
    Includes bibliographic references and index.
    ISBN 1-55916-004-7
    1. Egypt—Juvenile literature. I. Title. II.
Title: Egypt. III. Series.
    DS49.P27   1994
    916.2—dc20   93-47098
                          CIP
                          AC

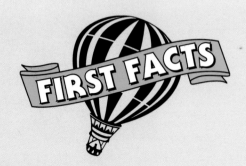

Egypt

. . . .

Official Name: Arab Republic of Egypt

Area: 386,660 square miles

Population: 77,505,756

Capital: Cairo

Largest City: Greater Cairo (15,842,400)

Highest Elevation: Gebel Katherina (8,652 feet)

Official Language: Arabic

Major Religions: Islam, Coptic Christianity

Money: Egyptian pound

Government: Republic

TABLE OF CONTENTS

Our Blue Ball—The Earth

The Earth can be divided into two hemispheres. The word hemisphere means "half a ball"—in this case, the ball is the Earth.

The equator is an imaginary line that runs around the middle of the Earth. It separates the Northern Hemisphere from the Southern Hemisphere. North America—where Canada, the United States, and Mexico are located—is in the Northern Hemisphere.

The Northern Hemisphere

When the North Pole is tilted toward the sun, the sun's most powerful rays strike the northern half of the Earth and less sunshine hits the Southern Hemisphere. That is when people in the Northern Hemisphere enjoy summer. When

the North Pole is tilted away from the sun, and the Southern Hemisphere receives the most sunshine, the seasons reverse. Then winter comes to the Northern Hemisphere. Seasons in the Northern Hemisphere and the Southern Hemisphere are always opposite.

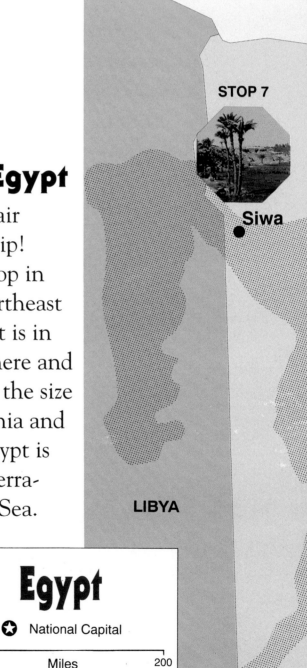

STOP 7

Siwa

LIBYA

Get Ready for Egypt

Hop into your hot-air balloon. Let's take a trip!

You are about to drop in on a country in the northeast corner of Africa. Egypt is in the Northern Hemisphere and is slightly smaller than the size of the states of California and Texas put together. Egypt is bordered by the Mediterranean Sea and the Red Sea.

Egypt

⭐ National Capital

0   Miles   200

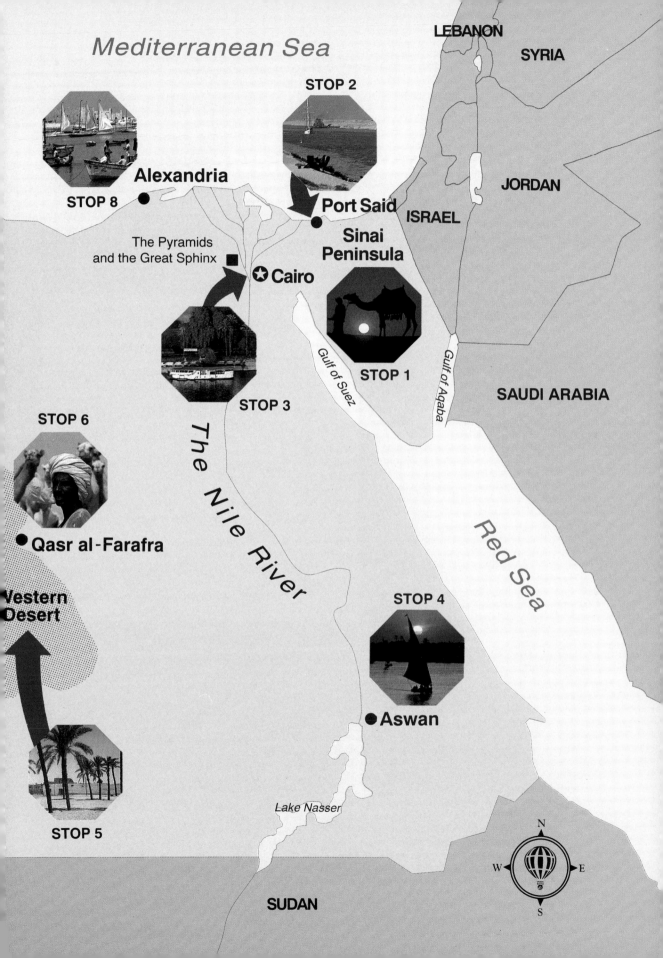

Mediterranean Sea

LEBANON

SYRIA

STOP 2

JORDAN

Alexandria

STOP 8

ISRAEL

Port Said

The Pyramids
and the Great Sphinx

Sinai
Peninsula

Cairo

Gulf of Suez

Gulf of Aqaba

STOP 1

SAUDI ARABIA

STOP 3

The Nile River

STOP 6

Red Sea

Qasr al-Farafra

STOP 4

Western
Desert

Aswan

STOP 5

Lake Nasser

N

W   E

S

SUDAN

Stop 1: Sinai Peninsula

Our first stop is the Sinai Peninsula. A peninsula is a land formation that has water on 3 sides. The Sinai Peninsula is separated from the rest of Egypt by the Gulf of Suez and the Suez Canal. The southeast coast of the peninsula is bordered by the Gulf of Aqaba. The Red Sea is just south of the peninsula.

A line of camels is led across the desert in the Sinai Peninsula.

Red and brown mountains cover the southern areas of the peninsula. The mountains are surrounded by desert plains. The northern area has sand dunes, swamps, and palm trees. Beautiful beaches of white sand line the shore.

Gebel Katherina, Egypt's highest mountain, is in the Sinai Peninsula. It rises 8,652 feet above sea level. Near this mountain is another tall mountain called Gebel Musa. This name means "mountain of Moses." It is also called Mount Sinai. In the Old Testament of the Bible, Moses received the Ten Commandments from God on Mount Sinai.

The Bedouin people live in the Sinai Peninsula. They are nomads, people who constantly travel from place to place. You might see the Bedouins riding their camels across the desert.

Now it is time to travel **north** to Port Said.

Stop 2: Port Said

Port Said is a busy seaport on the Suez Canal. The canal connects the Mediterranean Sea with the Red Sea. Ships that weigh as much as 150,000 tons pass through the canal. Huge ships and tankers line up at the north entrance of the canal at Port Said. Then the ships move through at less than 8 miles per hour. After about 15 hours, the ships complete their trip through the canal and sail into the Gulf of Suez.

Most of Port Said sits on an island. It is connected by bridges to the mainland. Port Said is a favorite stop for tourists. It has beaches along the Mediterranean Sea. You might like to swim in the warm water here.

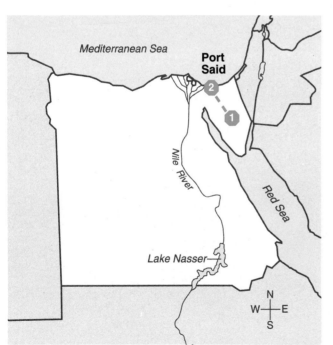

*Now we'll travel **southwest** to Cairo, Egypt's capital city.*

*A ship passes slowly through the
Suez Canal.*

Stop 3: Cairo

Cairo is on the Nile River. The Nile is the world's longest river. It is about 4,000 miles long. The Nile starts south of the equator in Africa. It flows northward through miles of desert. Then it empties into the Mediterranean Sea.

More than 15 million people live in Egypt's capital city. Cairo is a crowded, noisy city. It is also a city filled with things both old and new. Skyscraper hotels and tall office buildings are only a few blocks away from houses made out of mud and brick.

One area of the city is called Islamic Cairo. Islamic means "of Islam." Islam is an important religion in Egypt. In Islamic Cairo, there are many beautiful places of worship called mosques. These mosques tower against the sky.

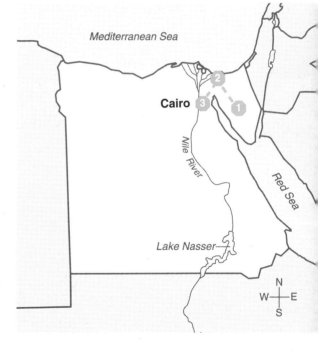

Opposite: The ancient city of Cairo lies along the banks of the Nile River.

The Pyramids and the Great Sphinx

The famous pyramids and the Great Sphinx are found in an area of Cairo called Giza. The Great Pyramids were tombs for the pharaohs, or kings. The Pyramid of Cheops is the oldest pyramid in Giza. This pyramid was built with more than 2 million limestone blocks and is 450 feet high.

The Great Sphinx also sits in the desert. The sphinx has the body of a lion and the head of a king. It was carved from one giant piece of limestone. It is about 240 feet long and more than 65 feet high. The Great Sphinx is thought to be a monument to Khafre, the pharaoh responsible for building the second great pyramid.

A Bedouin and his child travel through Giza to see the pyramids.

The head of the Great Sphinx towers above the desert.

Let's leave the pyramids and the Great Sphinx now and travel **southeast** to Aswan.

A felucca, or sailboat, gently glides across the Nile River at sunset.

Stop 4: Aswan

Aswan is the city farthest south in Egypt. It is on the Nile River. White-sailed feluccas (small boats) travel the river. They pass little islands that are covered with palm trees.

In Aswan, you can ride a horse-drawn cart. It can take you through groves of eucalyptus—tall, flowering trees. You can also ride through small, narrow alleyways and visit the outdoor markets. Here you might see some traditional dances being performed or hear musicians playing the music of ancient Egypt.

You may also want to visit the Aswan High Dam. The dam is more than 2 miles across. The water behind the dam creates Lake Nasser. It stretches 310 miles south of the dam. The dam creates electricity through its power plant. The water from the dam is also used to irrigate, or water, a million acres of farmland around Aswan.

Now let's travel **west** to the Western Desert.

Stop 5: Western Desert

Much of Egypt is covered by the Western Desert. The temperature may reach 125 degrees Fahrenheit. Even lizards do not come out in the noontime heat. Very few people live in the Western Desert. The people who do live there stay near an oasis. An oasis is an area in a desert that has a supply of water. There are several scattered across the Western Desert.

Kharga is the largest oasis. It has temples and palm trees. It also has the ruins of an ancient city. There are tombs and an underground walkway. Ancient Egyptians knew that the desert sun was dangerous and built this walkway for shade.

*Now let's travel **north** to a tiny oasis.*

A desert town sits among palm trees near the Kharga oasis.

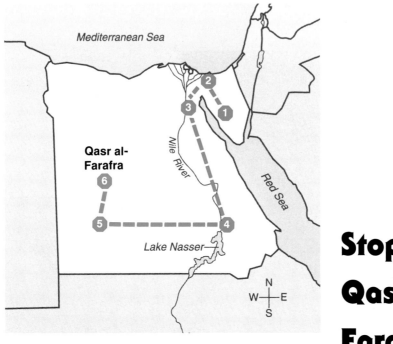

Stop 6: Qasr al-Farafra

Farafra oasis is the smallest oasis in the Western Desert. Its main town is Qasr al-Farafra. About 2,300 people live here.

Many of these people are Bedouin. In the past, most Bedouins were nomads who traveled across the desert. The Bedouins of Qasr al-Farafra are not nomads anymore, but they still follow many of the ancient ways of life. They live in small mud-brick houses that have wooden doors. The women sew their own dresses and shirts and go to a well to bring water to their homes. They carry the water in jugs on top of their heads. Some men are farmers who grow oranges, lemons, or olives. Olive oil is a major product of Qasr al-Farafra.

A camel driver herds his caravan through the Western Desert.

Just outside Qasr al-Farafra is the White Desert. The sands of this desert are blinding white. In this desert, there are rocks with strange shapes. It is hard to see the rocks against the bright sand. You may need to wear dark glasses to see them clearly.

*A different kind of oasis is to the **northwest**. We'll stop there next.*

Stop 7: Siwa

Siwa is a patch of green in the brown desert. About 12,000 people live in Siwa. This oasis is green because it has 300 fresh water springs. You will find thousands of date palms and olive trees here. Siwa is famous for its dates and olives. There are also many kinds of birds in the country-side. You might see quails and falcons in the sky.

The springs do more than provide water for crops. People also bathe in pools made by the springs. Cleopatra's Pool is a famous spring. It

comes out of a stone-brick pool. Another pool area is called Fantasy Island. It has palm trees and green bushes growing around it. The island sits in the middle of a salt lake.

Following their ancient ways, some women in Siwa rarely leave their homes. If they do, they wear gray, woolen robes that cover them from head to foot. The men in Siwa are different from men in other oasis cities. Here, the men carry water from the springs to their homes. This is usually a chore that only women do.

Fresh water from springs allows green grass and plants to grow in the middle of Egyptian deserts.

Growing Up in Egypt

Most Egyptian children attend Muslim public schools that start at 7:45 A.M. They line up for morning assembly in the school yard. After they sing the national anthem, they enter their school. When the teacher walks into the classroom, all the children stand up. Each class lasts 45 minutes. Students may study 3 languages: Arabic, English, and French. They also study math, science, social studies, music, and other subjects. Schools are closed on Fridays. These are holy days of rest in the Islam religion.

Muslim children pray several times a day. During the holy month of *Ramadan*, school starts at 9:00 A.M. Summer vacation is from May to September. Students get 2 weeks off for New Year's vacation.

Muslim men and boys pray together in a group called a *salat el'gomah*. Women and girls pray at home. The prayer lasts about 20 minutes.

Opposite: A young Egyptian boy walks near the Red Sea.

For our final stop, we'll travel **northeast** *to Alexandria.*

A steady stream of fishing boats travel in and out of Alexandria's busy harbor.

Stop 8: Alexandria

Alexandria is on the north coast of Egypt. The city is close to the Nile River and faces the Mediterranean Sea. The city was first built over 2,000 years ago. Now it is a city of more than 3 million people.

Alexandria is the major seaport of Egypt. Although it was built a long time ago, Alexandria is a modern city. It has colleges, libraries, parks, and office buildings.

The main area of Alexandria is Midan Saad Zaghloul. This is a large square near the harbor. Around this square are stores, restaurants, offices, hotels, and bus depots. Just south of the city is the Mahmudiya Canal. This canal is very important. It connects Alexandria to the Nile River.

You may want to visit the beaches in Alexandria. There is also a zoo with tigers and many other animals. You can take a 16-mile drive along the sandy shore. The view is breathtaking.

Food in Egypt

Fresh fruits and vegetables can be bought from vendors along the streets of Cairo.

When you get hungry in an Egyptian city, you can visit wonderful restaurants. You might order *ful medemmess*. This is a dish made by cooking *ful* (beans) until they are soft. Then they are served with olive oil, lemon, and salt. You scoop up the meal with *aysh*, round slices of whole wheat bread. You might also spread *tahini* on a slice of *aysh*. *Tahini* is ground up sesame seeds mixed with yogurt.

For dinner you can have *lahma-misabika*. This is stewed lamb and tomatoes. With the meat is served *farkha* (broiled chicken) and *mahshi*, a kind of spicy rice soup.

Now it's time to set sail for home. When you return, you can think back on the wonderful adventure you had in Egypt.

Glossary

eucalyptus A type of green, flowering tree or shrub that is widely grown in warm climates.

felucca A narrow, fast sailing boat.

irrigate To supply land with water by means of channels, streams, or pipes.

mosque A Muslim temple or place of worship.

nomad A member of a group or tribe that has no permanent home and travels from place to place.

oasis A place in a desert that is fertile because it has a supply of water.

peninsula A land formation that is surrounded by water on 3 sides.

pharaoh The title of a king in ancient Egypt.

Further Reading

Zuehlke, Jeffrey. *Egypt in Pictures*. Lerner Publications, 2003.

Gray, Shirley Wimbish. *Egypt*. Compass Point Books, 2002.

Webster, Christine, and Dahl, Michael. *Egypt: A Question and Answer Book*. Capstone Press, 2005.

Jackson, Elaine. *Egypt: Come on a Journey of Discovery*. QEB Publishing, 2004.

Suggested Web Sites

www.sis.goc.eg/
www.touregypt.net/
www.egypttoday.com/

Index

Acknowledgments and Photo Credits
Cover: ©Sylvain Grandadam/Photo Researchers, Inc. pp. 4, 6: National Aeronautics and Space Administration; pp. 10: ©Kathleen Campbell/Liaison International; p. 13: Linda Bartlett/Photo Researchers, Inc.; p. 14: ©Walter Leonardi/Gamma Liaison; pp.16, 18, 24: Egyptian Tourist Authority; p. 17: ©Kurgan-Lisnet/Liaison International; p. 21: ©Fred J. Maroon/Photo Researchers, Inc.; p. 23: Thierry Tinacci/Gamma Liaison; p. 26: ©F. & H. Schreider/ Photo Researchers, Inc.; p. 29: ©Jack Fields/Photo Researchers, Inc.; p. 30: ©Peter Beattie/Gamma Liaison.
Maps by Blackbirch Graphics, Inc.